Introduction to Embroidery

LILLIAN ROGERS

Cambridge University Press

CAMBRIDGE
LONDON   NEW YORK   MELBOURNE

This Series of books is designed to present the first essentials of Embroidery in a visual form. Each stage is illustrated by a drawing and careful explanation so that beginners can develop their skills stage by stage. The ideas this Series of books provide can be developed by individuals in a way that depends on their own particular skills and interests.

People using this Series of books as a preparation for examinations can mount samples of their work on coloured sheets of paper as worksheets for the purposes of assessment. When users have worked through the complete Series they will have a number of worksheets to show as an indication of the kind of work they can achieve.

Introduction to Embroidery describes the four basic groups of stitches, and gives simple examples of the variations that can be obtained by the use of looped stitches and chained stitches. It prepares the ground for *Embroidery: Working Stitches* and other later books in the Series.

Contents

Needles used in embroidery   2
Tools for embroidery   3
Threads used for embroidery   4
Four basic stitch groups   6
Looped stitches   8
Chained stitches   14
Blanket stitch sample   22
Exploded square sample   23
Geometric shapes as an inspiration for design   24
Exploded circle sample   29

Published by the Syndics of the Cambridge University Press
The Pitt Building, Trumpington Street, Cambridge CB2 1RP
Bentley House, 200 Euston Road, London NW1 2DB
32 East 57th Street, New York, NY 10022, USA
296 Beaconsfield Parade, Middle Park, Melbourne 3206, Australia

© Cambridge University Press 1977

ISBN 0 521 21179 4

First published 1977

Printed in Great Britain by
David Green (Printers) Ltd, Kettering, Northamptonshire

Needles used in embroidery

It is important to use the correct needle: crewel needles are used for general embroidery, and are made in various sizes from large to very fine and small, but for heavy materials and threads there are special needles, such as tapestry or chenille. For leather, a needle with a tapered honed point is used, and in fine beading you will require beading needles designed for this purpose.

Leather needle, or glover: the honed tapered point makes it easier to sew thick fabrics, particularly leather.

Crewel needles embroidery needles with long egg-shaped eyes to take several strands of threads

Chenille needles are short with large long eyes, used for thick threads on coarse fabric.

Sharps and betweens used for ordinary sewing, short round eyes, from long size to very short and fine

Tapestry needles have long large eyes and blunt points, which can slip through open-mesh material without splitting it. They are used with wool or thick embroidery cotton on canvas or open-mesh material.

Beading needles very fine, long to very short with a long eye. These needles are very fragile and used only to apply beads.

Darners very long needles with long eyes to take wool thread and span long distances

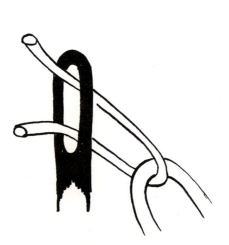

To pull a thick thread, such as wool, through the eye, loop cotton through the wool, thread the doubled cotton, and pull it all through the eye.

Tools for embroidery

There are some essential tools that are used frequently in embroidery, and it is useful to make a collection of these and keep them in your work-box. They include: a fine sharp pair of embroidery scissors, a thimble, a stiletto, a tracing wheel, some dressmakers' carbon paper, a roll of felt, a small tin of French chalk, a piece of tailors' chalk and several reels of thread, one of Sylko, one of tacking cotton and one of invisible nylon thread.

French chalk

Thimble

Stiletto
used for making holes for broderie Anglaise

Cutting shears

Embroidery scissors
small and fine-pointed

Water-colour paintbox and some fine brushes

Tracing wheel
used for marking designs through to fabric

Dressmakers' carbon paper

Felt roll: to use with French chalk in transferring designs with the prick and pounce method

Threads used for embroidery

There are a great variety of threads which can be used for embroidery: some are the traditional kind that are specially prepared, but there are many types of threads and wools that lend themselves very well to creative embroidery. It would be useful to collect odd lengths of rug and textured knitting wools. End thrums of weaving threads and string will give endless variety.

Stranded embroidery thread: can be separated into six single strands or used in groups, pulls straight, the skein has a definite lustre.

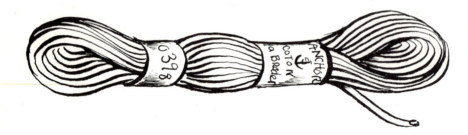

Coton à Broder: medium-fine thread, skein has to be opened and cut before use, slight lustre

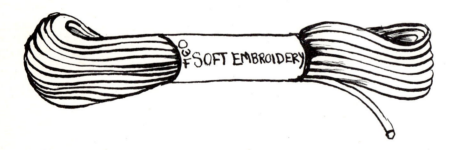

Soft embroidery thread: no lustre, medium-thick, is pulled out from the skein

Tapestry: wool embroidery thread, for use on canvas or wide-meshed fabric, can be pulled from the skein

Threads used for embroidery

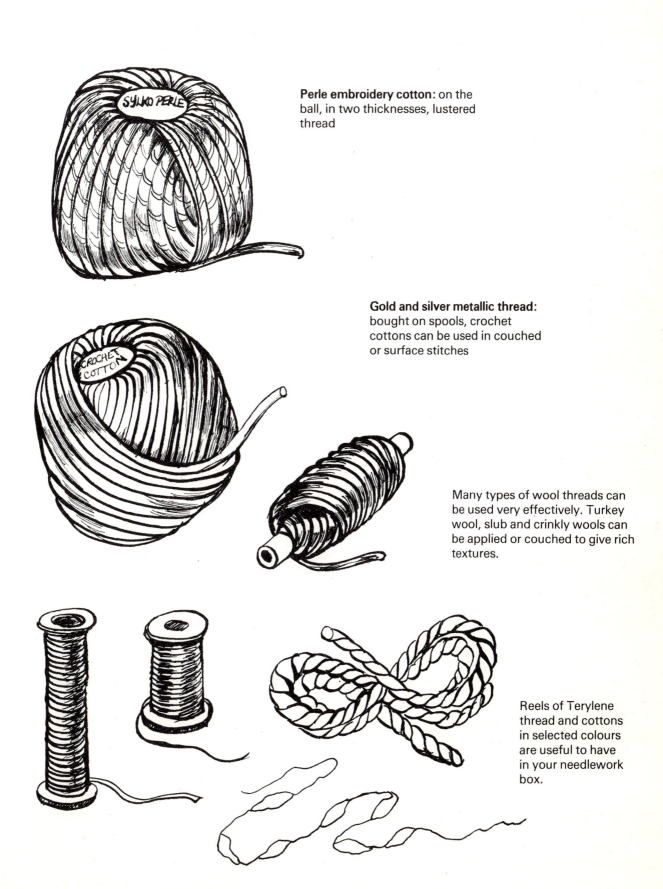

Perle embroidery cotton: on the ball, in two thicknesses, lustered thread

Gold and silver metallic thread: bought on spools, crochet cottons can be used in couched or surface stitches

Many types of wool threads can be used very effectively. Turkey wool, slub and crinkly wools can be applied or couched to give rich textures.

Reels of Terylene thread and cottons in selected colours are useful to have in your needlework box.

Four basic stitch groups

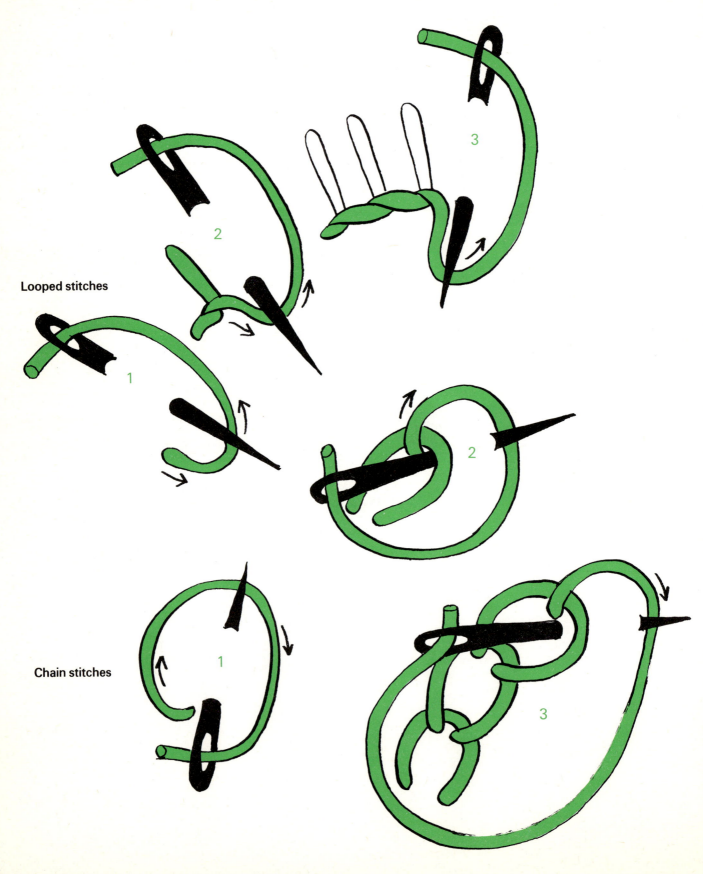

Looped stitches

Chain stitches

Four basic stitch groups

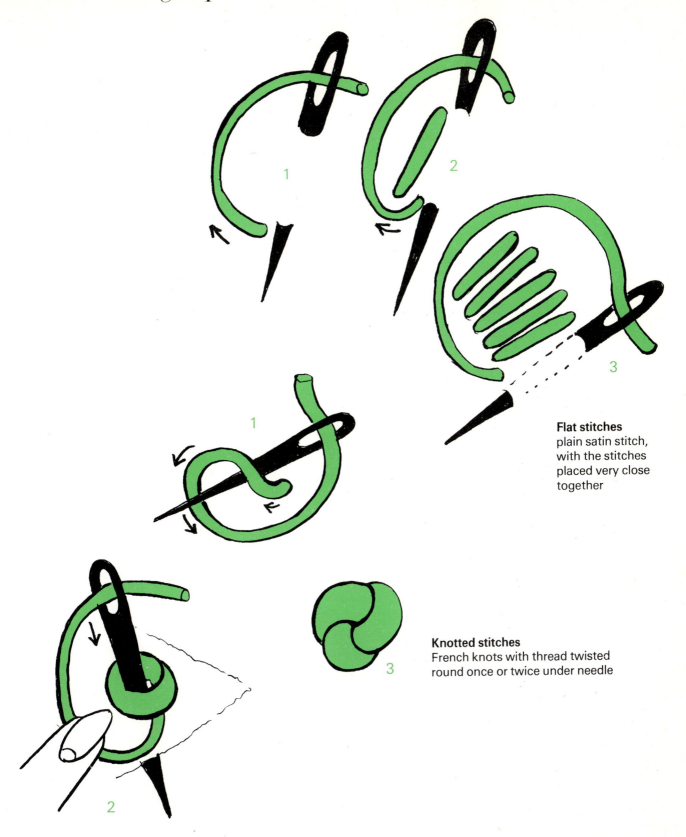

Flat stitches
plain satin stitch, with the stitches placed very close together

Knotted stitches
French knots with thread twisted round once or twice under needle

The following stitch sections show many variations of two of these four basic groups. They can be combined to make composite stitches once the basic stitches have been mastered, and the same stitch can be repeated with threads of different thickness to add greater variety and richness to embroidery design. Flat and knotted stitches are shown in **Embroidery: Working Stitches**, the next book in the Series.

Looped stitches

Blanket or buttonhole stitch: variations worked in threads of contrasting colours and varied thickness achieve a great variety of textures. Bugle beads can be slotted on the 'legs' of the stitches with a beading needle.

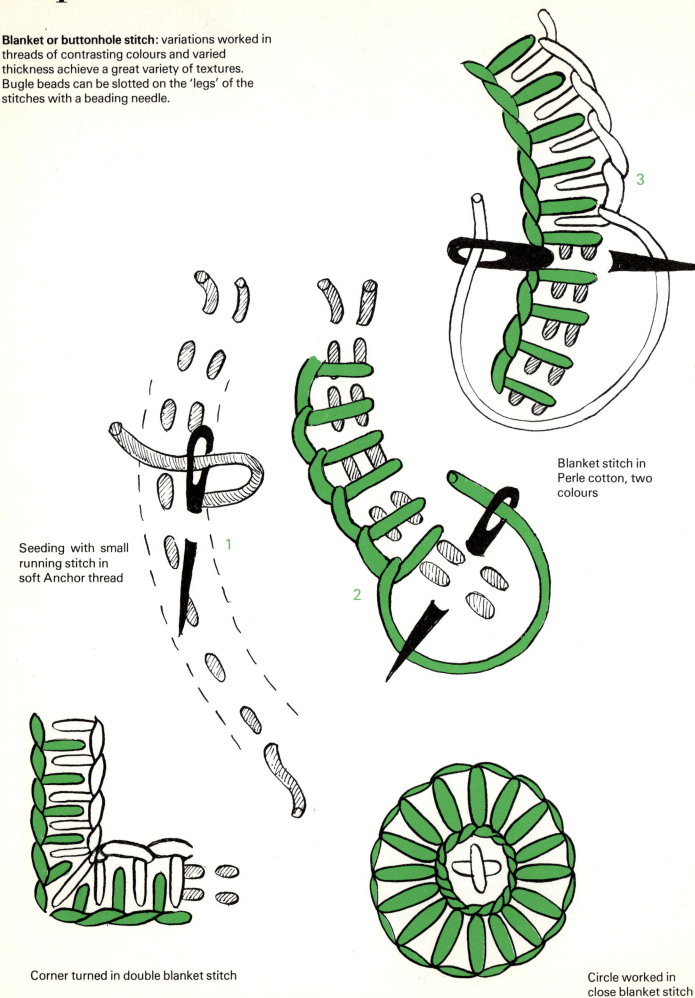

Seeding with small running stitch in soft Anchor thread

Blanket stitch in Perle cotton, two colours

Corner turned in double blanket stitch

Circle worked in close blanket stitch

Looped stitches

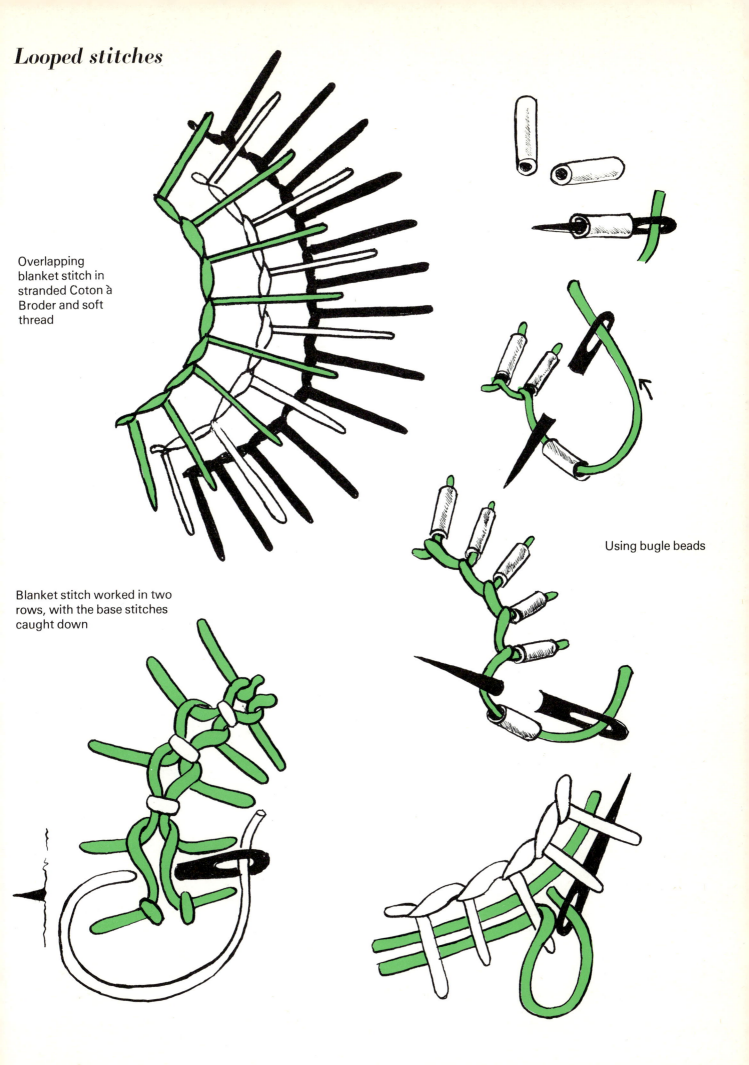

Overlapping blanket stitch in stranded Coton à Broder and soft thread

Blanket stitch worked in two rows, with the base stitches caught down

Using bugle beads

Blanket stitch in Coton à Broder, wool threaded under stitch bars

Looped stitches

Variations of blanket stitch worked in blocks of stitches, circles or alternating short and long stitches worked in groups

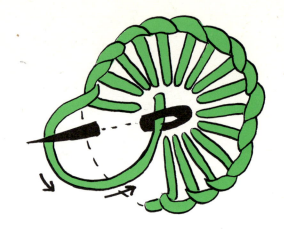

Circle worked from the centre

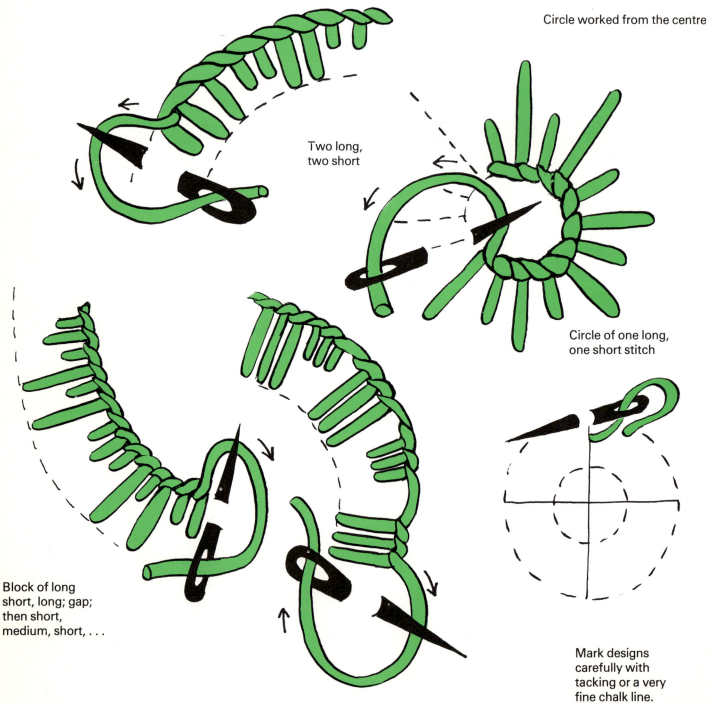

Two long, two short

Circle of one long, one short stitch

Block of long short, long; gap; then short, medium, short, ...

Blocks of three long, three short

Mark designs carefully with tacking or a very fine chalk line.

Looped stitches

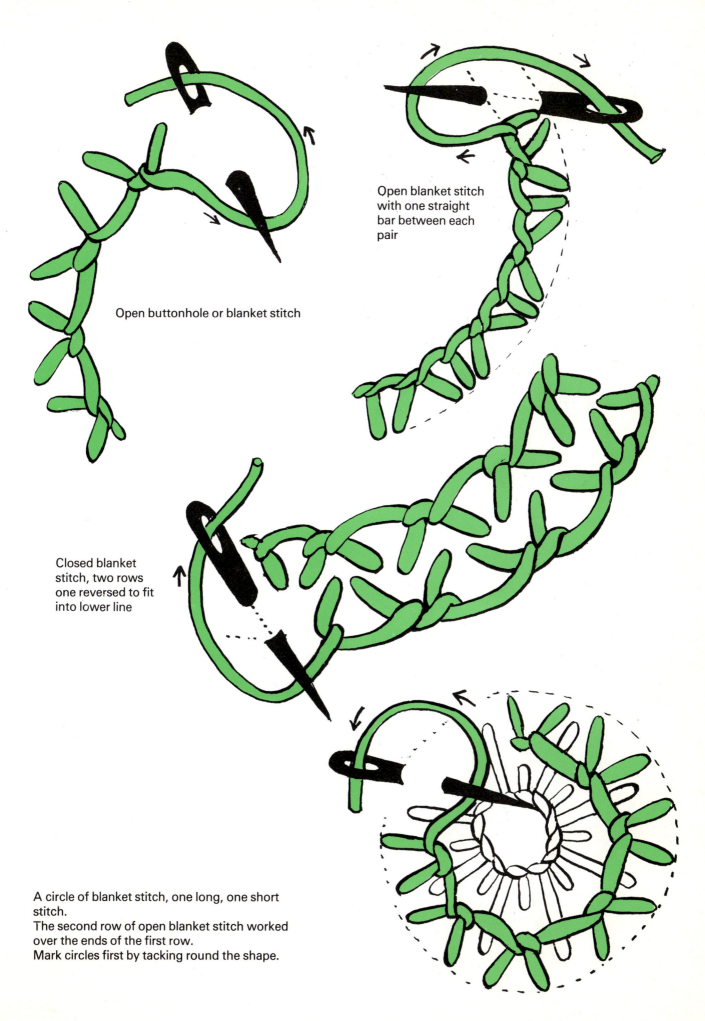

Open buttonhole or blanket stitch

Open blanket stitch with one straight bar between each pair

Closed blanket stitch, two rows one reversed to fit into lower line

A circle of blanket stitch, one long, one short stitch.
The second row of open blanket stitch worked over the ends of the first row.
Mark circles first by tacking round the shape.

Looped stitches

Fly and feather stitch are both part of the looped stitch group. There are many variations of these two stitches, which can be used to give close- or open-textured effects.

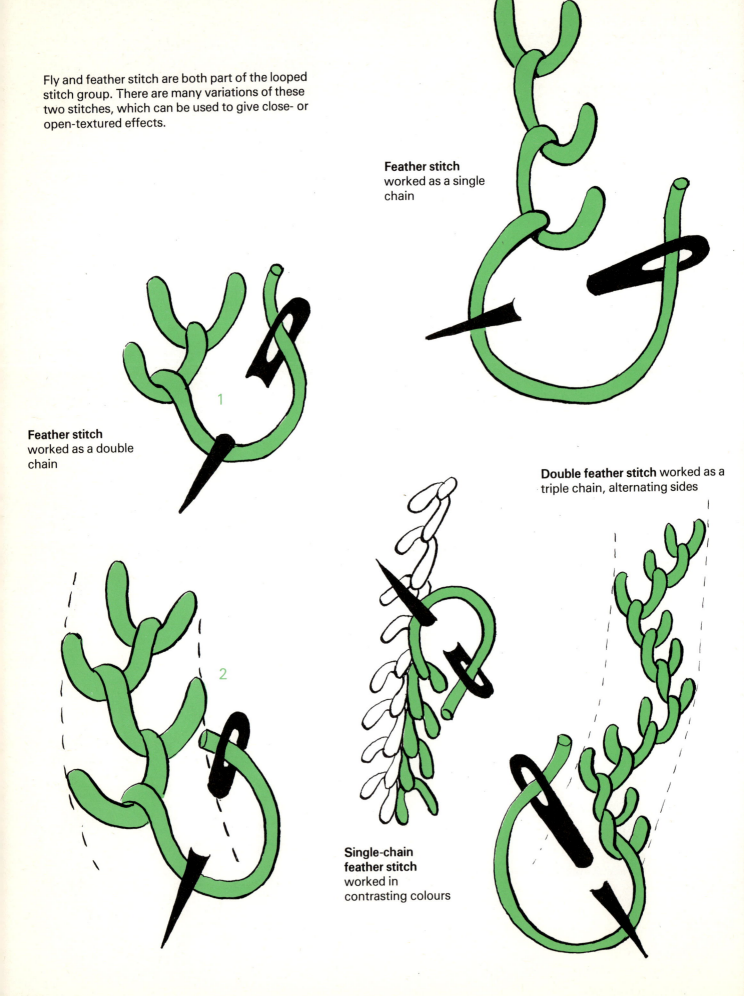

Feather stitch worked as a single chain

Feather stitch worked as a double chain

Double feather stitch worked as a triple chain, alternating sides

Single-chain feather stitch worked in contrasting colours

Looped stitches

Closed feather stitch: to start, bring needle out at arrow in stage 1.

Detached fly stitch worked in a circle, using contrasting colours or threads

Bring needle out at arrow in stage 1; the centre stitches should all be the same size, and the looped stitches should be parallel to each other.

Chained stitches

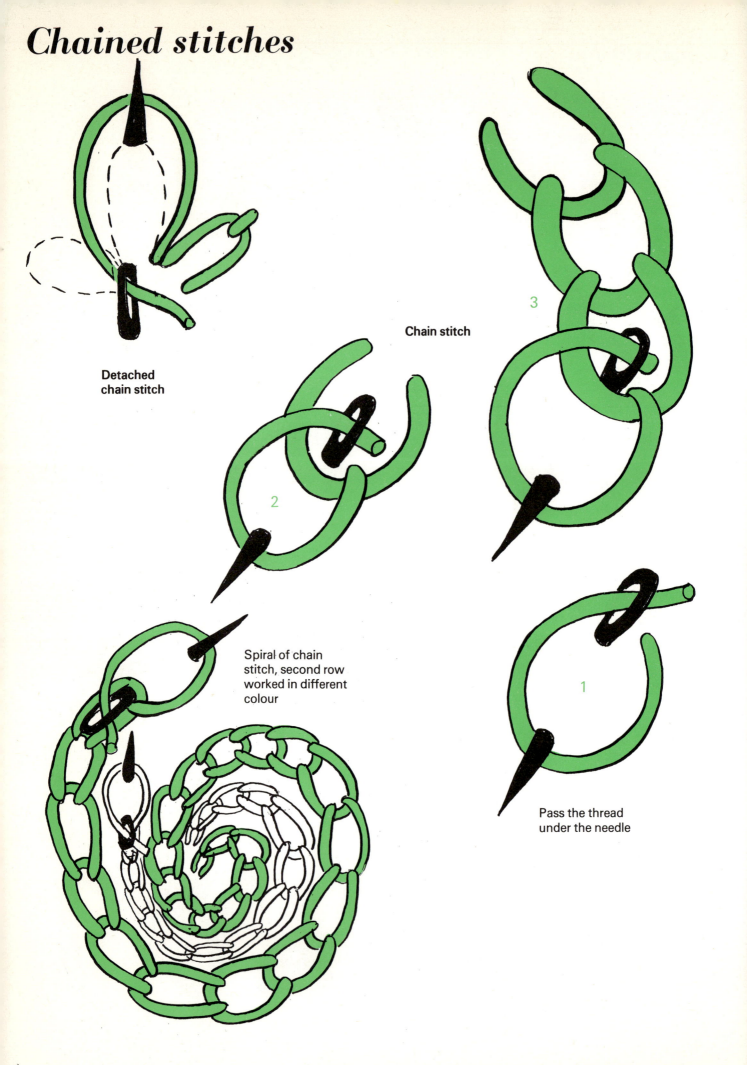

Detached chain stitch

Chain stitch

Spiral of chain stitch, second row worked in different colour

1 Pass the thread under the needle

Chain stitch is very versatile. There are many variations; the same stitch worked in a stranded thread and a wool gives a great variety of texture.

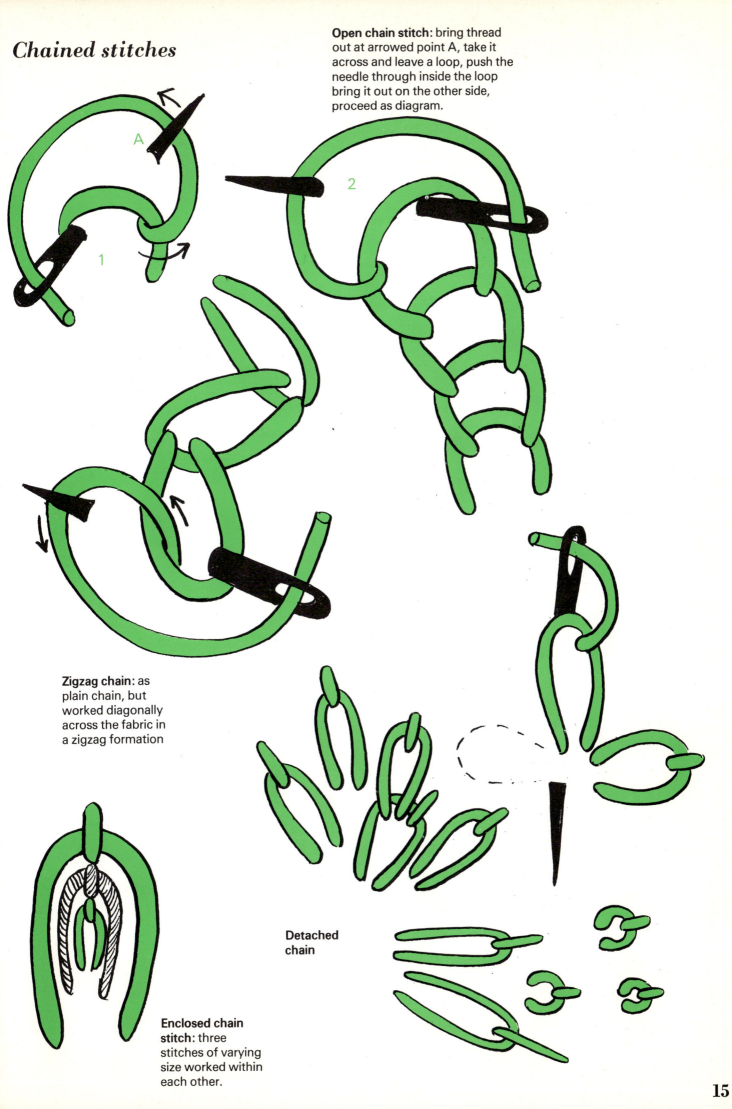

Chained stitches

Open chain stitch: bring thread out at arrowed point A, take it across and leave a loop, push the needle through inside the loop bring it out on the other side, proceed as diagram.

Zigzag chain: as plain chain, but worked diagonally across the fabric in a zigzag formation

Enclosed chain stitch: three stitches of varying size worked within each other.

Detached chain

Chained stitches

These are cable chain stitches, a little more complicated than plain chain, but if the diagrams are followed carefully, step by step, they can soon be mastered.

Bring the thread out at arrow, twist the thread around the needle, take up the stitch, passing the thread under the needle.

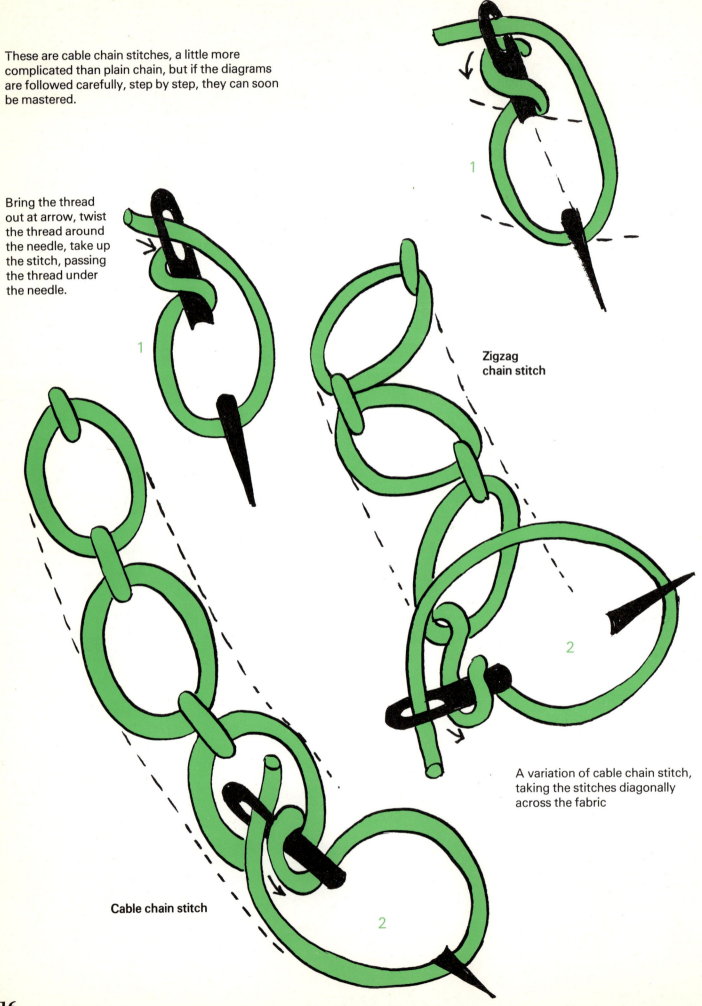

Zigzag chain stitch

A variation of cable chain stitch, taking the stitches diagonally across the fabric

Cable chain stitch

Chained stitches

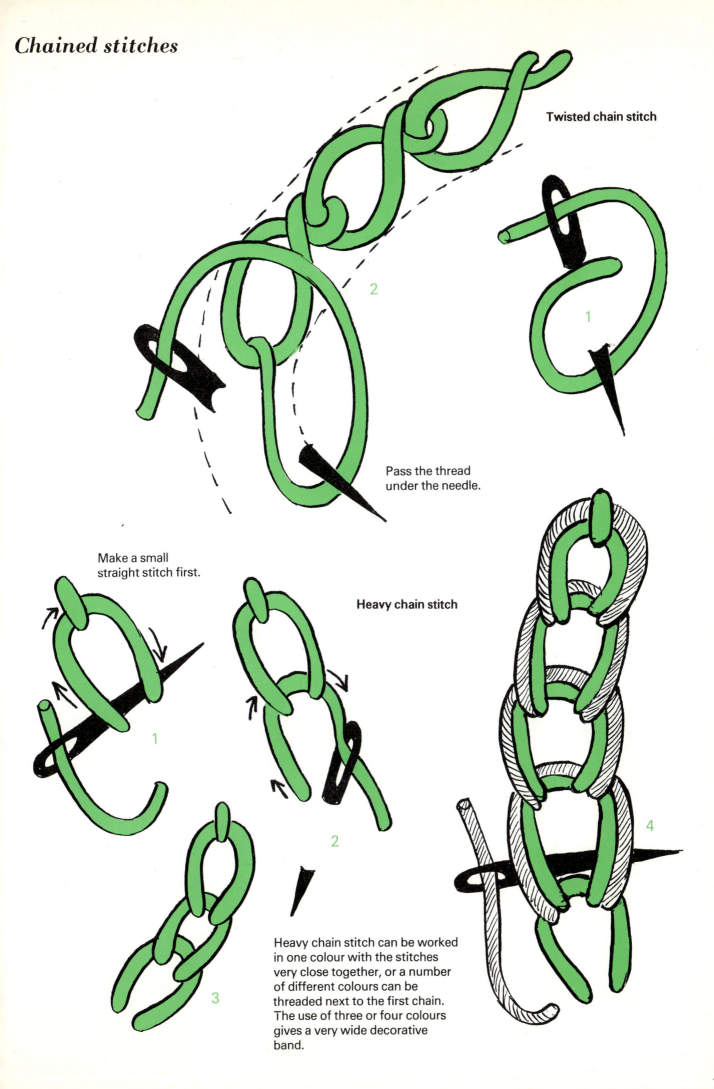

Twisted chain stitch

Pass the thread under the needle.

Make a small straight stitch first.

Heavy chain stitch

Heavy chain stitch can be worked in one colour with the stitches very close together, or a number of different colours can be threaded next to the first chain. The use of three or four colours gives a very wide decorative band.

Chained stitches

Rosette chain stitch and braid stitch are similar, and give a very rich effect. They are easier to work if two lines of tacking are laid down first, for the width of the finished row of stitches.

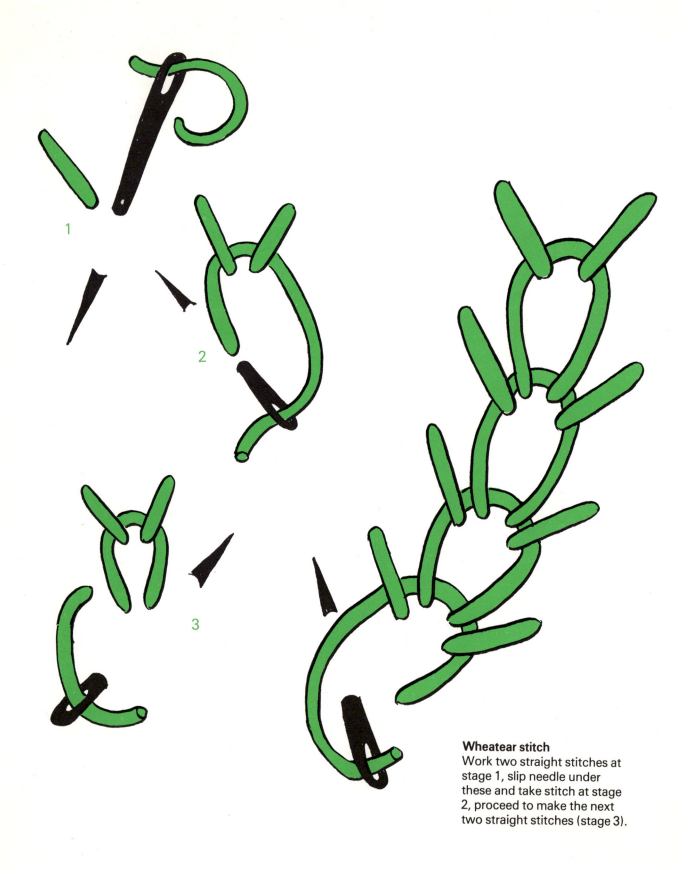

Wheatear stitch
Work two straight stitches at stage 1, slip needle under these and take stitch at stage 2, proceed to make the next two straight stitches (stage 3).

Chained stitches

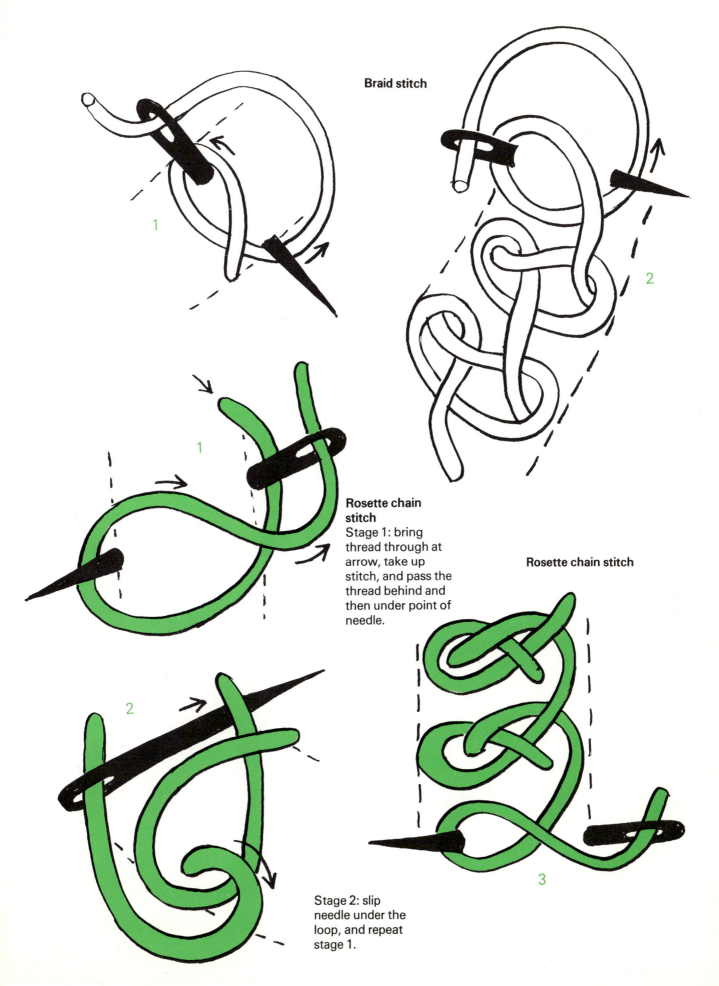

Braid stitch

Rosette chain stitch
Stage 1: bring thread through at arrow, take up stitch, and pass the thread behind and then under point of needle.

Stage 2: slip needle under the loop, and repeat stage 1.

Rosette chain stitch

Chained stitches

Detached chain stitches arranged in groups can be built up into motifs and further enhanced with the use of sequins and bugle beads, if the finished article is suitable for this type of decoration.

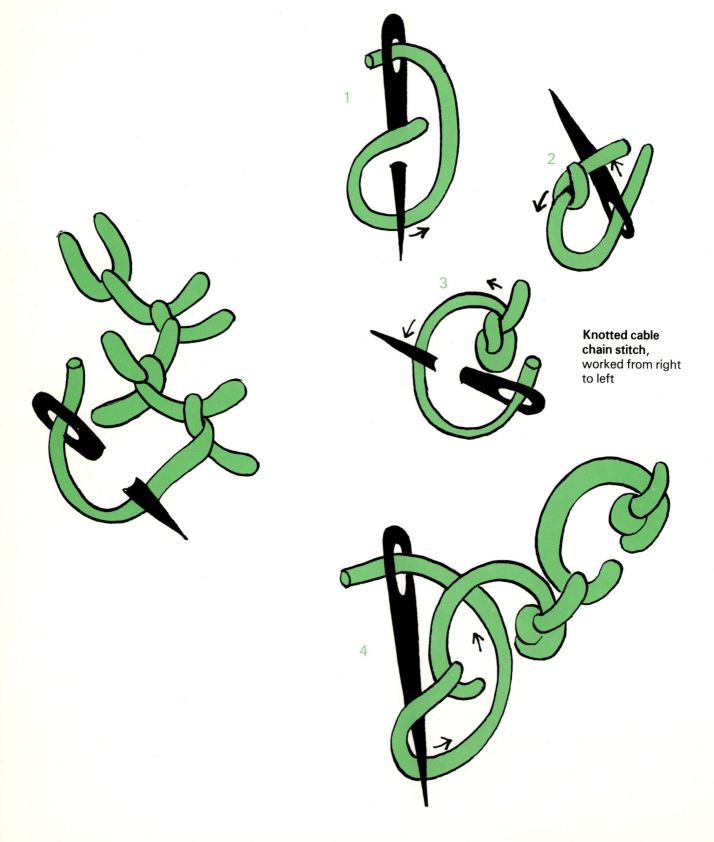

Knotted cable chain stitch, worked from right to left

Chained stitches

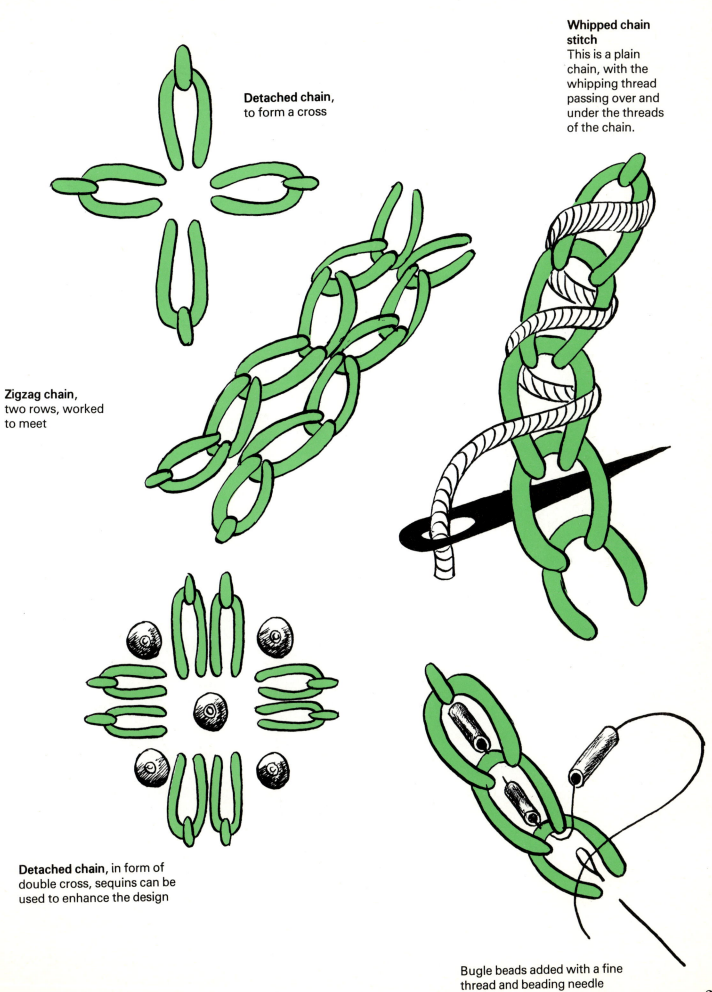

Detached chain, to form a cross

Whipped chain stitch This is a plain chain, with the whipping thread passing over and under the threads of the chain.

Zigzag chain, two rows, worked to meet

Detached chain, in form of double cross, sequins can be used to enhance the design

Bugle beads added with a fine thread and beading needle

Blanket stitch sample

Exploded square sample

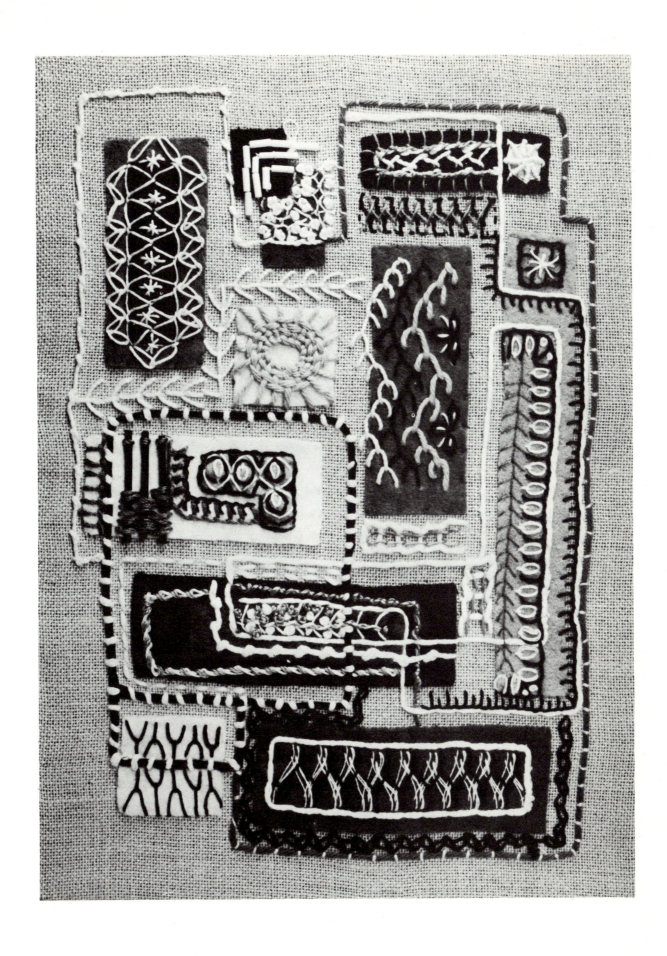

Geometric shapes as an inspiration for design

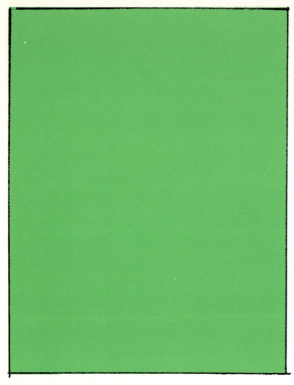

Cut rectangle in paper.

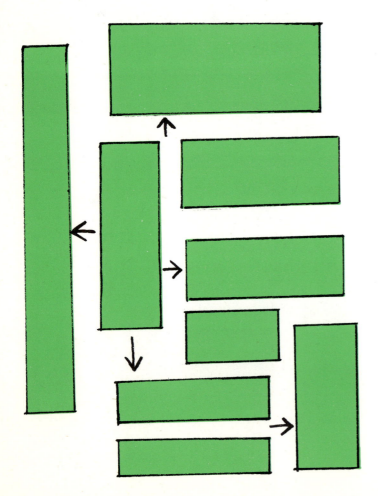

Exploded rectangles or squares

Mark out coloured paper, cut and expand the design, stick the coloured paper on a plain sheet.

Draw in design lines, working in overlapping rectangles, showing arrangement and shapes of suggested stitches.

Geometric shapes as an inspiration for design

Design for exploded rectangle or square

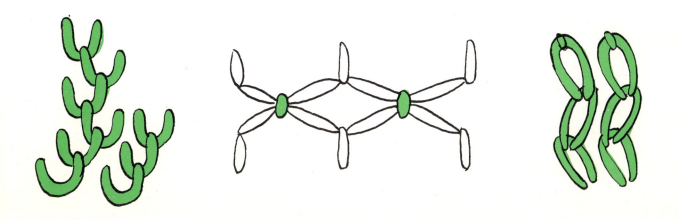

Geometric shapes as an inspiration for design

Cut triangle in coloured paper.

Exploded triangle

Mark out design, cut and expand the shapes; stick the coloured paper onto a plain background.

Draw in design lines, using triangle and diamonds as base, show arrangement of stitches.

26

Geometric shapes as an inspiration for design

Design for exploded triangle

27

Geometric shapes as an inspiration for design

Design for exploded circle

Exploded circle sample

Geometric shapes as an inspiration for design

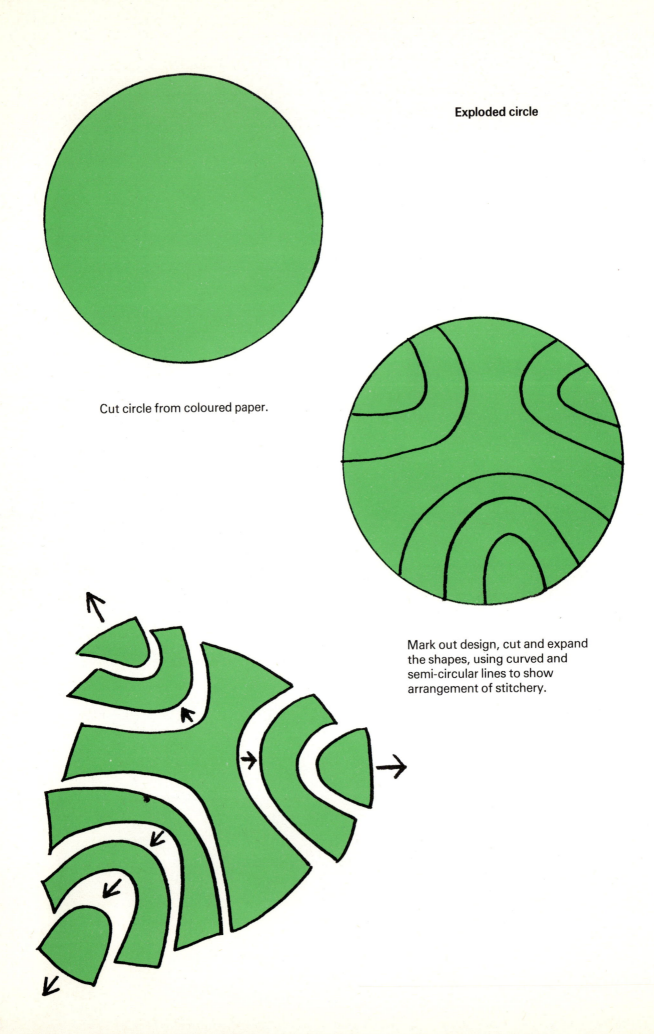

Exploded circle

Cut circle from coloured paper.

Mark out design, cut and expand the shapes, using curved and semi-circular lines to show arrangement of stitchery.

Geometric shapes as an inspiration for design

Design for exploded circle

Geometric shapes as an inspiration for design